Self Portrait With His Dog *(detail)* - 1745 - Oil on canvas, 90 x 70 cm London, Tate Gallery.

HOGARTH

"By a fluent genius he designed and invented freely...particularly some caricatures of several persons or affairs. Afterwards, without copying other paintings or old masters, by his perception and forceful judgment he became surprisingly fast the master he now is."

John Vertue

William Hogarth was born in London in 1697 and died there in 1764. His life and work were both, in the truest sense, metropolitan, despite a few trips into the country or abroad. London was nearly always to be the setting of his scenes, its character shaping his art. He has always been renowned as a satirist, his engravings and prints proving immensely popular, but he was also a powerful portraitist. Above all, although indebted to French art, he helped to establish English painters as really equal to foreign artists.

Before Hogarth, English art was derivative and provincial. After him, a school of portrait and landscape painters emerged which would rival any in Europe. Yet Hogarth himself was primarily concerned with neither of these forms, making a living chiefly through his engravings.

Making a living was something his father, a school-master and hack writer, had signally failed to do, spending long periods in Fleet Street debtors' prison. Such early poverty may have given Hogarth a bitter view of the

world; it certainly deprived him of a full education. Instead, he was apprenticed at the age of 14 to an incompetent silver plate engraver, Ellis Gamble, to learn a trade for which he lacked the patience to excel. Throughout his twenties, Hogarth lived by engraving cheap designs for books or shopcards, including an elegant example for himself (page 6).

Hogarth's first success came with *The Taste Of The Town,* or *Masquerades And Operas* (page 4), published in 1724. It shows a street scene in which crowds flock either to a masquerade or to a harlequin show, while a barrow-load of the works of the great English dramatists like Shakespeare is carried off for waste-paper. In the background, three fops admire a pediment on which William Kent, the fashionable young architect of the new Palladian style which Hogarth strongly disliked, looks down on the statues of Michelangelo and Raphael. Hogarth's message is clear: false new tastes are supplanting proper appreciation of the old masters. Such attitudes

Self Portrait - 1732 - Sketch from a travel album - London, British Museum.

Engraving from The Analysis of Beauty, *the essay on aesthetics which Hogarth published in 1753.*

linked Hogarth with the conservatism of the painter Sir James Thornhill, who had decorated the inside of the dome of Saint Paul's Cathedral. Thornhill's baroque style was then being eclipsed by the Palladian fashions, brought back from Italy by Lord Burlington.

The Taste Of The Town, although a success, had brought Hogarth little money and about this time he decided to start painting in oils. This was a momentous step for someone with no proper training but Hogarth brought it off triumphantly. The series of paintings that followed, especially those illustrating Grey's satirical *Beggar's Opera,* starting in 1728, (page 4) show a new-found mastery of oil-painting which struck his contemporaries as miraculous.

As if to celebrate his success, Hogarth eloped with Thornhill's 19-year old daughter Jane - the only note of personal drama in his otherwise very quiet personal life. The couple never had any children. They were soon reconciled with Sir James who introduced Hogarth to wealthy patrons. For these he painted family

portraits such as *The Cholmondeley Family* which revealed his skills as a painter of portraits. Hogarth then hit upon a novel idea - painting and then engraving "modern moral subjects" in a series of vividly satirical scenes of daily life.

A Harlot's Progress (1731) and *The Rake's Progress* four years later (pages 6-8), depict the rise and fall of flawed but not inherently evil characters. In their differing circumstances - the young country girl who, seduced as she steps off the coach, slides into prostitution and then into prison; the young heir who fritters away his petty fortune and ends in madness in Bedlam - both show up the vanity of fashionable pleasures, with a fine mixture of the tragic and the comic. The engravings made of these scenes, sold mainly through bookshops, were enormously popular; but pirated editions of *A Harlot's Progress* robbed Hogarth of much of his hard-earned reward.

Because of this, Hogarth lobbied hard for the Copyright Act of 1735, which for the first time gave engravers and writers real control over their works; he delayed the publication of *The Rake's Progress* until the Act had been passed. Now Hogarth could sell his engravings to a wider public, so making his name and finally banishing the spectre of poverty.

When Thornhill died in 1734, Hogarth inherited not only his house but also his clients. He joined the Sublime Society of Beef Steaks, a club both political and literary. In it, and in London's numerous coffee houses, Hogarth spent many hours, meeting writers like Swift, Richardson and Fielding. This was the great age of English satirical journalism and Hogarth enjoyed its virulent attacks on social or political corruptions.

Portrait-painting was also important to Hogarth throughout his life, as can be seen in his

The Bench - 17 x 20 cm - *reproduction of an engraving of 1758*

Sarah Malcolm Executed in Fleet Street March 4 1732 for Robbing the Chambers of Mrs Lydia Duncomb in ye Temple and Murdering Her, Elis: Harrison & Ann Price

Portrait Of Sarah Malcolm *(reproduction from an engraving of 1733 - 17.5 x 16 cm). She was hung for the murder of three people. Hogarth visited her in prison and painted her portrait in oils, from which this engraving was subsequently taken.*

"mighty portrait" of Captain Coram (page 14). This, combining French elegance with robust English honesty, was partly intended to boost the status of English portrait painters against the foreigners so often preferred by the aristocracy.

Hogarth's distaste for foreign affectations and people (reinforced by two unhappy trips to France in 1744 and 1748) surfaces clearly in *Marriage A La Mode* (pages 18-23), six "moral" works executed in 1743 which may be his masterpieces. They brim over with acute comic observation on every aspect of contemporary life, from the prevalence of Italian opera singers, whom Hogarth deplored, to the hypocrisy of puritans, whom he also despised. But, despite his comic exuberance, this meaningless way of life, with its marriage for money, empty pleasure-seeking and fashion-following is revealed as more tragic than comic.

For all his castigation of vicious foreigners, the influence of the French Rococo in *Marriage* is inescapable; Hogarth in fact employed French engravers for the mass-production of his engravings, grudgingly accepting their technical superiority. The graceful curves of the light-hearted Rococo derived from the Baroque but were less pompous. *Marriage A La Mode* was a success, both financially and critically, for Hogarth. But, following the example of writers whom he knew like Henry Fielding or Samuel Richardson, he switched from attacking the follies of the modish world to praising the simple pleasures of the virtuous in *The Happy Marriage* (page 26).

Hogarth not only turned from satire; he contributed to the world of artistic theory with his own views entitled *The Analysis Of Beauty* (page 2), published in 1753, in which he explained his aesthetic theory based on the serpentine line of beauty and the superiority of curves to angles. "Simplicity without variety is insipid", he declared. Besides attacking again the rigid Palladians and praising Christopher Wren, he dismissed Van Dyck's popular, elegant portraits. Such pugnacious views found more support among clergymen than among fellow artists.

In 1757, his appointment to the post of Serjeant Painter to the King was seen by some as a betrayal of his radical ideals. The last years of his life were not happy ones for Hogarth. He quarrelled with old friends like John Wilkes, the radical, savaging him in a brilliant etching in 1762. The dilettante Horace Walpole, who visited the painter that year, thought he was going mad. Hogarth, however, died sane if embittered in the city he had so frequently and wittily depicted on 25 October 1764.

THE BEGGAR'S OPERA

1731 - Oil on canvas, 56 x 72.5 cm
London, Tate Gallery

This painting shows a scene from *The Beggar's Opera* by the playwright John Gay, with music by J. Christoph Pepush. It was a vivid, colourful representation of the London underworld, both a parody of the formal Italian style of opera popularised by the foreigner Handel, the court's favourite composer, and a political satire on government corruption. The opera, first performed at the Theatre Royal in Lincoln's Inn Fields in January 1728, was a tremendous success. This was a great stroke of luck for Hogarth, for such satire exactly fitted his now burgeoning talents. The first production of *The Beggar's Opera* took place in January 1728. Within 18 months Hogarth had painted no less than five versions displaying his new-found mastery of oil painting. This painting of 1731 is a replica of the fifth, now at Yale. The Prime Minister Robert Walpole had recognised himself among the thieves and crooks depicted by Gay and asked George II to prevent the staging of the sequel to the opera, which would have been called *Polly*.

Hogarth here illustrates the culminating point of the opera, the second scene of the third act. The highwayman Macheath is about to be hanged in Newgate prison which has been faithfully reconstructed on the stage. On the left Lucy Lockit kneels in front of her father the gaoler, while on the right Polly Peachum, also kneeling in front of her father, begs for the prisoner's life to be saved. In a reversal of the normal roles, Macheath looks braver and nobler than his opponents. Hogarth painted several recognisable notables among the spectators, including the Duke of Bolton on the far right.

Masquerades And Operas, engraving by Hogarth, printed in 1724 13 x 30 cm. In this engraving, Hogarth openly attacked Lord Burlington who was very keen on the Italian operas of Handel, besides being the greatest proponent of the Palladian style of architecture, also Italian in origin. The pedimented gateway in the background supports a statue of the architect William Kent, Burlington's protégé, and epitomises the type of new foreign architecture Hogarth so hated. In the foreground, a pregnant woman carts off the books of great English playwrights (Shakespeare, Congreve, Ben Jonson) in a wheelbarrow, shouting: "Waste paper for shops!" The new taste championed by Lord Burlington encouraged mindless masked balls and operas (according to Hogarth). Following the trend, theatre companies were abandoning the great dramatic or comic writers of English theatre.

Drawing (1728) by Hogarth, inspired by John Gay's The Beggar's Opera Windsor, Royal Library.

THE RAKE'S PROGRESS: THE RAKE'S LEVEE

1733-34 - Oil on canvas, 62.5 x 75 cm
London, Sir John Soane's Museum

Immediately after the success of *A Harlot's Progress*, Hogarth started working on a new "moral" series describing the rise and fall of a Rake. The series consists of eight paintings or episodes: *The Young Heir, The Levée, The Tavern Scene, Arrested For Debt, Marriage To An Old Heiress, In A Gaming House, The Debtor's Prison,* and finally *Bedlam* (the madhouse).

Tom Rakewell, the Rake, is the son of a miser who has built up a small fortune; this his heir determines to spend as splendidly as possible, moving to London where he hopes to buy his way into high society. *The Levée* shows the Rake, elegantly established in London, besieged by a chorus of grotesque figures offering all sorts of unnecessary but expensive services, to help him ape the manners of the nobility. Foreigners are represented by the composer playing music from Handel's new opera *The Rape Of The Sabine Women*. In the print, the opera cast-list cascading down the back of the musician's chair shows the names of many noted castrati singers as rapists - a typical Hogarthian absurdity; castrati (eunuchs) are unlikely to rape Sabine women.

In the centre a fencing-master brandishes his foil with its deadened tip, fencing being another of the aristocratic attributes Rakewell seeks to acquire. Tom Rakewell himself, in his night cap, holds a note in his hand. In front of him a monkey-like dancing master poses on the balls of his feet; behind him an architect proffers a plan of a proposed garden, yet another extravagance.

The Rake is surrounded by all the worst temptations of London; clearly he is going to succumb.

The Rake's Levée, reproduction of an engraving of 1735, 31 x 39 cm. This print reproduces the scene with the same orientation as the painting, having been produced by placing the painting in front of a mirror or working from a reversed copy of the painting. The artist wanted to reproduce exactly the original poses of the characters.

HOGARTH THE ENGRAVER
On 25 April 1720, Hogarth published this notice, advertising the fact that he had set up as an independent engraver. At first he only found work reproducing cheap designs but engraving was to become his lifelong occupation. His production over his lifetime was vast: 256 signed engravings, 38 others based on his drawings and carried out under his supervision, and a further 38 which may be his. Hogarth's income depended mainly on engraving throughout his life, so it took precedence over his painting. He often painted in order to engrave from his paintings. Further, when he thought that there was a market for a subject he had already painted, he engraved it so as to reproduce it in large quantities. There are engravings of almost all the paintings on these pages, the image naturally normally being reversed compared with the painting.

THE RAKE'S PROGRESS: ARRESTED FOR DEBT

1733/35 - Oil on canvas, 62,5 x 75 cm
London, Sir John Soane's Museum

This is the fourth scene in the tragi-comedy of the Rake's career. The third had shown him carousing in The Rose tavern in Covent Garden, a notorious brothel.

He is shown at the very moment of his arrest for debt. The episode is set in St James' Street, with the gates and battlements of the royal palace in the background, and surrounded by the traffic of sedan chairs and carriages.

Hogarth has added new details and characters to the engraving 32 x 39 cm. The chief characters are the same as in the painting, but lightning can be seen forking symbolically in the sky, while the boy stealing the walking stick has been replaced by a group of urchins, stealing and playing cards.

The unfortunate rake is being carried in a sedan chair to the Levée which Queen Caroline used to hold on her birthday (1 March) at St. James's Palace, in the hope of a post at court to restore his ruined fortune. Despite the sedan's drawn curtains, he is recognised by two baillifs who show him a warrant for his arrest. A young woman, the seamstress Sarah Young who loves him, comes to his help by offering to pay, so securing his freedom. Hogarth does not spare anyone, whatever their class: on the left, for instance, an urchin steals the Rake's walking stick as he emerges from his chair while the lamp lighter above drips some oil on his wig, perhaps not by mistake. The incident is watched by a man on the right who, like one of the baillifs, must be Welsh, since there is a leek on his hat, as is the custom in Wales on Saint David's Day, March 1. Such precise details give Hogarth's paintings their individual character.

The fifth scene of A Rake's Progress, Marriage To An Old Heiress, Oil on canvas, Sir John Soane's Museum, takes place in the church of St. Marylebone, then on the outskirts of London, known for its clandestine weddings. The Rake is clearly marrying the ugly old woman for her money, rejecting Sarah Young, who is trying to get into the church in the background, holding his baby.

THE DISTRESSED POET

Detail - 1736 - Oil on canvas, 63.5 x 78.5 cm
Birmingham Museum and Art Gallery

Grub Street, that infamous but mythical London street where miserable hack writers struggled and failed to make a living, was an aspect of London Hogarth knew only too well from his impoverished childhood. Alexander Pope, who was as ferociously satirical a poet as Hogarth was a painter, had attacked the whole tribe of incompetent poets and unperceptive critics in his satirical masterpiece *The Dunciad,* published in 1728. In the engraving Hogarth made from this painting, he added these lines from *The Dunciad* at the bottom:

"Studious he sate, with all his books around

Sinking from thought to thought, a vast profound!

Plung'd for his sense, but found no bottom there;

Then writ and flounder'd on in mere despair."

This is a poet's garret in an extreme state of chaos. At the centre of the picture, a woman is busy sewing and mending her husband's threadbare breeches.

The room around her is absurdly untidy with clothes and papers littering the floor, a sword lying on the floor and a dog, who is taking advantage of the situation to sink his teeth into the only food left to eat. On the wall, the cupboard stands open and bare.

On the right, the milkwoman has just burst in to present her bill to the wife, demanding payment. The poet, meanwhile, is staring out through the window, apparently unaware of what is happening around him. He is scratching his head over a poem entitled, ironically, *Poverty.* The general poverty contrasts strongly with the elegant wig and dressing gown of the poet.

In the painting The Distressed Poet, which is printed here complete, Hogarth condemns the detachment of the artist who has all the negative qualities of a poet - incompetence, dreaminess, poverty - without possessing the essential genius which alone would make it all worthwhile.

The Enraged Musician, engraving published in 1741, 33 x 40 cm. Hogarth here depicted another struggling artist. As with the poet, the elegant wig and costume reveal someone who wants to be creative in order to rise in the world, but who, as is clear from his surroundings, has so far had no success. He is shown leaning out of the window, stopping his ears as he tries to silence the noisy local inhabitants.

THE STRODE FAMILY

1738 - Oil on canvas, 87 x 92 cm
London, Tate Gallery

Hogarth here gave the well-established genre of the conversation piece a typically English feel. The family is shown having breakfast or tea. From left to right are Dr Arthur Smyth, a sombrely-dressed cleric who was to become archbishop of Dublin in 1766, William Strode an MP, the butler Jonathan Powell, Lady Anne Strode, wife of the MP and eldest sister of the sixth Earl of Salisbury, and Colonel Samuel Strode, brother of William.

William Strode (1712-55) came from a wealthy and well-connected family of South Sea brokers. He had married Lady Anne Cecil in 1736 and a son William was born 23 July 1738, so the absence of any sign of children suggests a date at the beginning of 1738.

When the painting was X-rayed in 1984, it became clear that there had been considerable changes in its composition: the bookcase at the back had originally been a formal, nobly pedimented doorway, while William Strode originally leaned forward over the table to the right,

The composition is based on the half-circle in which the characters have been arranged. The static quality of the scene is relieved by the figure of the butler who links the two pairs of characters, standing very nearly in the centre of the picture. The two dogs on either side add a typically Hogarthian note and close off the circle.

gazing towards his brother. This was a commissioned piece and it shows Hogarth painting something close to a flattering, or at least pleasing, portrait. Both the young MP and his military brother look very fine in their gold-braided coats, while Dr Smyth, the future archbishop, has a suitably other-worldly air, his eyes raised heavenwards. Lady Anne is carefully poised with her teacup. Even the Italianate canvases on the walls are depicted without burlesque.

Doctor Smyth, the future archbishop of Dublin, is depicted by the artist staring into space, presumably thinking about what he has just read in *the book he is holding in his right hand. William Strode, the Member of Parliament, seems to be inviting him to have some tea. Lady Anne has a* *cheerful, pink rosy complexion, matching her pink and white clothes; Colonel Strode closes the scene off by standing majestically posed.*

PORTRAIT OF CAPTAIN CORAM

1740 - Oil on canvas, 239 x 147.5 cm
London, Foundling Hospital

This is probably the grandest of Hogarth's portraits, and certainly the one of which he was most proud, boasting about its unsurpassed qualities in later years. Captain Coram was a philanthropist of note. A retired naval officer, he had been appalled by the sight of hundreds of children who were abandoned in the streets of London, with nothing to look forward to but lives of crime and early deaths. With donations from some rich but caring citizens, Coram set up the Foundling Hospital in 1739, where these children would be educated to become seamen or apprentices - useful members of society. Hogarth himself made a large donation to the Hospital and was one of its first governors; he and his wife (who were childless) became foster-parents to some of the children - proof that the savage satirist had an actively kind side to him.

The Hospital was also important to Hogarth for it was the first place to display permanently works by exclusively British artists.

The structure of this painting may derive from French courtly models, especially the portrait of Samuel Bernard by Hyacinthe Rigaud, who was also shown seated by a balustrade overlooking the sea with a globe beside him. But Captain Coram's rosy, friendly face is very distinctly English. Equally, while Samuel Bernard was painted in all his silken finery, complete with medals and sash, Captain Coram is shown in well-cut but plain English clothes, befitting the kind of honest Englishman Hogarth admired.

The scroll under Captain Coram's right arm bears the words "The Royal Charter" referring to the hospital's recent foundation.

Anthony Van Dyck: Portrait Of Cardinal Bentivoglio (detail) 1625 - 196 x 146 cm - Florence, Pitti Palace. Hogarth was aware of the Flemish tradition but did not admire Van Dyck, then considered a master portraitist. Van Dyck's imposing but hyper-elegant courtiers were exactly the sort of portraits he detested. Hogarth painted his solid Portrait Of Captain Coram as a challenge to such courtly painters. Note especially the contrast between Bentivoglio's long, thin hands and Coram's solid, square ones.

J. Zoffany: Don Ferdinand Of Bourbon (detail) - 1778 - 107 x 86 cm - Parma, Galeria Nazionale. Hogarth's portraits had little influence either in England or abroad. Instead, painters like Johann Zoffany, who came to England from Germany about 1760, were far more popular. Zoffany catered to the general desire for elegant, flattering portraits, emphasising gorgeous clothes, as here. The only real similarity between Don Ferdinando and Captain Coram is in their poses and their red coats.

The Royal Charter

THE SHRIMP GIRL

Detail - c. 1740 - Oil on canvas, 63.5 x 52.5 cm, London, National Gallery

This is a particularly lively and charming study from real life, rare in that Hogarth seldom let himself be carried away by such fresh innocence in a girl. This beautiful shrimp girl (the picture was probably going to be used as a model for an engraving) has been sketched using touches of light colours applied directly to the canvas, without the outline being drawn first. This technique has produced a work of great charm, freshness and spontaneity, qualities which could easily have been lost in a more finished painting.

In his *Analysis Of Beauty* of 1753. Hogarth demanded: "Who but a bigot will say that he has not seen faces and necks, hands and arms in living women that even the Grecian Venus doth but coarsely imitate?" Hogarth believed passionately that the true standard of beauty was set by nature, not by antique art, and that observation was therefore the key to painting. Real art should be about real life and the main objects of study should not be "the stony features of a Venus" but "a blooming young girl of fifteen".

The Shrimp Girl embodies this ideal perfectly. The pupils of her wide open eyes sparkle with life and her smile expresses extraordinary vitality and freshness. This shows Hogarth could respond deeply to genuine innocence.

Portrait of Mrs Salter - 1744 - Oil on canvas, 76 x 63.5 cm - London, Tate Gallery. Another woman's portrait by the artist, one of the most elegant he painted. He has succeeded in conveying the character of the sitter by paying great attention to the details of her clothes and her pose. In spite of - perhaps because of - its finished aspect and the soft nuances of its colours, this portrait has less freshness and spontaneity compared with The Shrimp Girl.

The diagrams show the various phases in the evolution of Hogarth's work. He worked straight onto the canvas with the brush, using pale, diluted colours which allow the canvas to show through. On a prepared canvas, he first spread the pale colours of the face, the bust and the background; then he applied the other colours for the clothes, hat and basket; finally, he completed the work by adding the luminous touches of the white of the veil and the black of the hair and eyes which give her such a pert and lively expression.

MARRIAGE A LA MODE: AFTER THE MARRIAGE

1744 - Oil on canvas, 68.5 x 89 cm
London, National Gallery

Marriage A La Mode was a series of six episodes (*The Marriage Contract, After The Marriage, The Quack Doctor, The Countess's Levée, The Death Of The Earl,* and *The Death Of The Countess*) in which Hogarth depicted the tragic consequences of a marriage of convenience - for money, not for love.

This second scene is devoted to a moment in the young couple's home life. But without love, there is no real home life. The grandeur and luxury of the rooms (decorated in that pompous Palladian style Hogarth constantly attacked) are marred by the squalor and disorder everywhere apparent. The clock shows that it is after midday but the Earl has only just returned from a night of debauchery. He sprawls, miserable and exhausted, on his chair; his sword lies on the floor, broken in some tavern brawl. It looks as if he has lost heavily at gambling. But he has undoubtedly also spent the night with another woman because the ribbons and material of a woman's underwear are spilling out of his pocket. The dog, as always in Hogarth's art,

making a point, sniffs at them. The servant in the background is showing a disgraceful lack of attention to his employers and is even more sloppily half-dressed than the Earl or Countess. Clearly, this is a very badly-run household.

The pictures on the walls are a jumbled and thoughtless collection of pieces both religious and secular, a scene from the god Jupiter's love-life crassly hanging between pictures of saints in the further room. The same lack of discrimination is apparent on the mantelpiece; in front of the painting of Cupid playing the pipes stands a Roman bust with ineptly repaired nose. Around this imperial Roman are scattered incongruously some Oriental amulets and figures, in taste as bad as the extraordinary clock which is decorated with a kitten at the top, fishes at the side and a Buddha-like figure at the base. All depict a vulgarity unrelieved by wit or taste.

The pitiless morning light streaming in harshly defines every detail. As usual, Hogarth has crammed his canvas with revealing points.

Marriage A La Mode: The Wedding Contract, *engraving of 1745, 35 x 44.5 cm. The first episode in the series, this is the marriage contract between a penniless nobleman, father of the young fop on the right, and a rich City heiress. It shows a situation typical of England in the 18th century: the alliance between the commoner who has grown rich by trade, but lacks style, and the aristocrat, proud of his titles but bankrupt.*

MARRIAGE A LA MODE: THE COUNTESS' LEVEE

1744 - Oil on canvas, 68.5 x 89 cm
London, National Gallery

Levées, where a lady of the house would receive callers whilst half-dressed and doing her toilet, were common among the 18th century aristocracy but not among the middle classes. In this fourth scene, the young countess has clearly accepted all the manners of her new rank without totally understanding the implicit rules of conduct governing her new position, as will become clear later.

Hogarth parades a string of characters or caricatures. The castrato singer, who may represent Giovanni Carestini, the idol of high society, trills away, plunging the picture's central figure, a typical opera lover, into ecstasy. She takes no notice of the cup of coffee being offered her by the black servant. The effeminate figure next to her is also in ecstasy, a fan dangling from his wrist; he seems to be trying to beat time with his hand.

A little further back, the seated figure with the whip, which indicates that he is a simple country gentleman and presumably the husband of the opera-loving lady, has fallen asleep bored. The character with his hair in paper curlers perhaps represents the Prussian diplomat Michel. The man playing the flute may be the German musician Weidemann.

Above this dubious group are some equally dubious pictures, the bottom one depicting the *Rape Of Ganymede,* referring covertly to the sexual proclivities of the effete foreigners beneath it. As always in Hogarth, foreigners are frauds if not worse. On the other side of the picture another black boy (black boys were then very fashionable as servants) is playing with a grotesque collection of objects with which houses were then decorated.

The Countess' Levée *is preceded by the episode* At The Quack Doctor's *(engraving of 1745), which takes place on the premises of a quack known all over London for his dishonesty and charlatanry. Here the young Lord Squander is accompanied by a pretty young girl, presumably his mistress of the moment. Sitting on a chair, he waves his stick while demanding tablets (to cure syphilis or procure an abortion?) The young girl is crying and the Earl appears to be taking it out on the other woman. She reacts by opening a knife and threatening to slash him. The decoration of the room is full of allusions to the disreputable, even superstitious, side of medicine: on the left, ropes with hooks and pulleys, toothed wheels and presses; in the middle, a half-open cupboard full of skeletons and anatomical figures; on the right, a worm-eaten skull resting on the table.*

Then comes the most important part of the painting. The Countess sits in front of a mirror while a Swiss servant is doing her hair. Lying languidly on the sofa, the corrupt lawyer Silvertongue expounds eloquently on some legal scheme whose details he holds in his hand. Above him and the Countess, erotic pictures in the style of the cinquecento painter Correggio - *Jupiter And Io, Lot And His Daughters* - hint at the true nature of this relationship between lawyer and noblewoman. For, neglected by her husband, the Countess' affections have been fatally caught by this smooth lawyer.

Henry Fielding, the novelist, called Hogarth a "comic history painter". The style which Hogarth invented, although popular with the public, was not really appreciated by the critics, who thought that only "tragic" historical painting could be taken seriously. One reason why Hogarth failed to impress may have been the very sweeping nature of his xenophobia and satires. Not all foreigners were corrupt or foolish.

The drama grows in the fifth episode The Death Of The Earl - 1744 - Oil on canvas, 68.5 x 89 cm - London, National Gallery. The Earl surprises his wife with her lawyer, now her lover, Silvertongue in a hired room at the dead of night. He tries to run him through with his sword, but Silvertongue succeeds in grabbing hold of the weapon and mortally wounding the Earl. While her husband collapses, the countess falls on her knees to beg his forgiveness, aghast at what has happened. The noise or perhaps a zealous neighbour has alerted the Watch who are coming in through the door while the murderer, still in his nightshirt, flees through the window. The final scene, The Death Of The Countess, reveals her back in her father's house, dying unloved.

The dramatic emphasis with which Hogarth painted these scenes shows the influence of the stage on his work. Significantly, Hogarth called the episodes of all his moral series "scenes" as in a play. The dramatic lighting - only two feeble sources of light to illuminate the tragic scene - and the way he seems catch the moment just before the curtain falls also have a theatrical flavour.

Hogarth portrays a gallery of absurd individuals. Among these is a ludicrous figure sporting curling papers in his hair (like little horns). The Prussian diplomat Michael, famous for his debauchery, is perhaps the model. The Swiss hairdresser, typically repellant, tends the hair of the Countess with gestures which by their affectation reveal he is not English. The little black boy is playing with a weird collection of objects one of which is significant: a statue of Actaeon (the mythical Greek prince turned into a stag by Artemis, the goddess of hunting, and torn to pieces by her hounds because he spied her bathing naked with her nymphs). Actaeon's horns symbolise the Earl's future cuckoldry and, through his own fate, the Earl's and Countess' dooms. Note that all the objects which the black boy handles have clearly just been bought; they still have auction numbers.

DAVID GARRICK AS RICHARD III

c. 1745 - Oil on canvas, 190.5 x 250 cm
Liverpool, Walker Art Gallery

Hogarth was only very occasionally able to obtain commissions for portraits outside his own circle of predominantly literary acquaintances. But he could sometimes attract patrons who wanted unusual portraits for particular purposes. He also sometimes started portraits speculatively, which was in fact the case with this immense picture. It was accepted once finished by the great Shakespearean actor who was never, of course, adverse to some extra publicity.

This is not strictly speaking a portrait, for it combines two genres - history painting and portrait. Hogarth made several later attempts at the Grand Manner, treating heroic or classical themes, of which the most famous is *Sigismonda* of 1758, not generally considered a masterpiece. Hogarth painted nothing more exactly like this; later in the century painting by other artists in the Grand Manner on subjects taken from Milton or Shakespeare became more common but this picture is significant for revealing another side of Hogarth's career - his attempt to paint in the grand style.

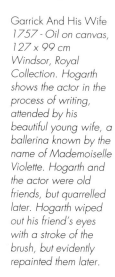

Garrick And His Wife 1757 - Oil on canvas, 127 x 99 cm Windsor, Royal Collection. Hogarth shows the actor in the process of writing, attended by his beautiful young wife, a ballerina known by the name of Mademoiselle Violette. Hogarth and the actor were old friends, but quarrelled later. Hogarth wiped out his friend's eyes with a stroke of the brush, but evidently repainted them later.

Strolling Actresses Dressing In A Barn, engraving of May 1738. Hogarth, who knew so much about the theatre and actors, has here produced a poignant scene. The contrast between the reality of life for an unremarkable acting company like this (far removed from the brilliant career of a Garrick) and the glamorous illusions they display on stage epitomises human vanities. A crown, in the bottom right, is being used as a table for a baby's feed; in the centre foreground a kitten plays with an orb. This is no satire but a sympathetic depiction of a group of unsuccessful actresses.

THE HAPPY MARRIAGE: THE BALL

1745 - Oil on canvas, 68.5 x 90 cm
London, South London Art Gallery

Hogarth began working on this painting soon after - and in reaction against - *Marriage A La Mode.* Probably he was influenced by the success of the illustrations a rival Joseph Highmore had made for Fielding's novel *Joseph Andrews.* It was meant to be part of a series now lost and known only through sketches, which charted the path of virtue. Soon after, he was to contrast the differing fates of the good and the bad with the *Industry* and *Idleness* series of engravings.

The Ball is unfinished and it is not known what it was meant to illustrate but this does not detract from its charm. The chandeliers are the most fully finished part; the light they shed contrasts with the moonlight shining gently on the bald head of the man mopping his brown by the bay window.

Hogarth's essential aim was to establish clearly the relationship between light and dark, as this is a night scene. He has painted the attitudes of the dancers very freely but produced a tremendous sense of rhythm. It seems almost possible to hear the lively dance music coming from somewhere offstage, so to speak.

Such exuberance among the dancers - the boy in the right foreground is whirling around wildly - suggests a rather unsophisticated but not inelegant gathering, perhaps in the country. The ancient nature of the room - no trace of fashionable Palladian splendours here; instead old-fashioned leaded windows - reinforces such conjecture about this unknown ball.

The composition makes the theatrical character of the painting obvious. It is arranged like an actual stage framed by the balcony and the figures on the left, and by the vertical element on the right.

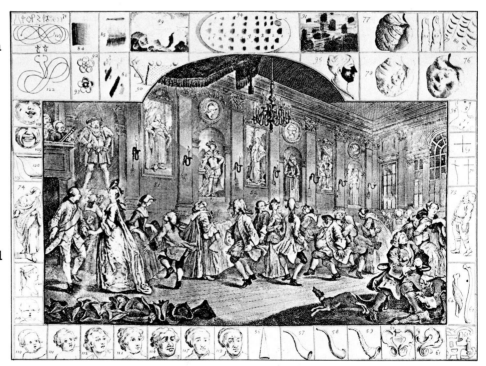

The most striking aspect of The Ball is the way in which the artist has succeeded in conveying the sense of movement. In his essay The Analysis Of Beauty (1753), from which this illustration is taken, Hogarth explains that "to render a ball in paint always demands an element of brute force and ridicule, even in the most elegant situations, because each figure is carrying out a suspended action rather than a completed movement: so that, if it is possible in the course of a dance to fix the performers at a particular moment, as one has to do precisely in a painting, less than one in 20 will have an agreeable position in spite of everyone's efforts to move gracefully. Otherwise the ensemble would seem incomprehensible." The first couple on the left express the graceful ideal, while the others illustrate the concepts of pause and movement with enclosing, broken or angular serpentine lines.

Hogarth's artistic (as well as personal) xenophobia did not extend to the Dutch tradition. In Dutch painting he hailed a similar honest, unpretentious concern with observation from nature, as opposed to the slavish emulation of antique or contemporary French and Italian art, then so fashionable. In particular, in his later portraits he sometimes show surprising parallels with the unadorned humanity of Rembrandt's great portraits.

This collection of six heads is in a most unusual format, evidently painted for his own pleasure, with no bodies or poses to distract from the characters so vividly depicted. Rembrandt's influence should not be seen as an "imitation" of a former master in the typical 18th century sense, in which the sitter dons 17th century costume. It is shown rather in the emphasising of personality through the technical means of chiaroscuro (contrasting light and shade), playing on the faces of each of the sitters.

Nothing could be more honest or human than these portraits. Even the boy at the top escapes the rigid lack of naturalism which normally makes Hogarth's pictures of children stiff and a little odd.

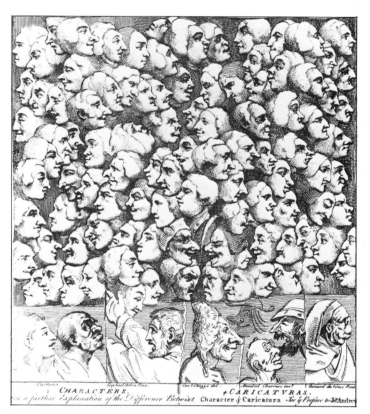

Hogarth devoted much time to studying facial expressions. These two prints are an example. In Characters And Caricatures of 1743 (above), hundreds of profiles are superimposed, seen from one side or the other, giving an example of every kind of human face. The lower section is devoted to faces copied from sketches by Raphael, Leone Leoni, Annibale Caracci and Leonardo da Vinci. Hogarth paid homage to the old Italian masters when in their proper place.
The Laughing Audience, 1733. For an acute observer of mankind such as Hogarth, the interest of a theatre lay not just in the performance itself, but in the auditorium, among the spectators who had come to enjoy the show. Here he has skilfully drawn every kind of laughter and mirth.

THE SCOURGE OF PRETENCE

Hogarth lived through the great age of satire in England, which was also - not coincidentally - the Age of Reason. Satire was, however, usually a literary phenomenon, its greatest exponents being writers like Jonathan Swift (1667-1745) or Alexander Pope (1688-1744). Both were Tories (sympathetic to the deposed Stuart dynasty), both opposed to the Whig nobles who dominated the government under the first two Georges (German-born and German-speaking monarchs, who cared little about England). The Whigs, whose government was led for 20 years by Robert Walpole (Prime Minister after 1721), practised political and financial corruption on a hitherto unknown scale to buy support - in Parliament, in the City of London or in the country. To boost their already immense wealth, these Whig grandees were not averse to marrying into the richest of the City merchant families, as in *Marriage A La Mode*. In the arts they favoured foreign artists and the new, pedantic Palladian style in architecture brought back from Italy by Lord Burlington in 1719. Above all, they had little concern for the world outside their own gilded, exclusive circles. The beggars who obstructed the wheels of their coaches were whipped out of the way. The society these nobles created may have been the most elegant Britain has known; it was also in many ways the most heartless. The strong and the lucky prospered, the weak went to the wall.

To Tory writers like Swift or Pope, who recalled the less corrupt and less callous rule of the Stuart monarchs (at least as seen in

HOGARTH AND HIS TIMES

	HIS LIFE AND WORKS	HISTORY	ART AND CULTURE
1697	Born in London 1 November	Peace of Ryswick ends War of the League of Augsburg against France. Louis XIV acknowledges William III as king of Britain	Birth of Canaletto Pierre Bayle: *Dictionary*
1712	Is apprenticed to the silver engraver Ellis Gamble	War of the Spanish Succession continues Tax imposed on books and newspapers in Britain in attempt to curb political satires	Birth of Jean-Jacques Rousseau Alexander Pope: *The Rape Of The Lock*
1720	Sets up as an independent engraver, scraping a living	South Sea Bubble bursts in Britain; thousands of investors ruined Russians invade Sweden Collapse of John Law's system in France creates financial chaos	Jean-Antoine Watteau: *The Sign Of Gersaint* Pope translates *The Iliad*
1721	First success with *The South Sea Bubble*	Peace of Nystad gives most of Sweden's Baltic empire to Russia Robert Walpole becomes Prime Minister; starts deep corruption in British politics	Charles-Louis Montesquieu: *Persian Letters* Death of Grinling Gibbons John Vanbrugh building Seaton Delaval
1725	Starts teaching himself to paint in oils, which leads to success with *The Beggar's Opera*	Death of Peter the Great of Russia	Antonio Vivaldi: *The Four Seasons* Nicholas Hawksmoor builds Christchurch, Spitalfields
1729	Elopes with Jane Thornhill, daughter of Sir James Thornhill	First Methodist meetings in Oxford	Henry Fielding: *Tom Thumb* Jonathan Swift: *A Modest Proposal* J.S. Bach: *Saint Matthew's Passion*
1731	Starts *The Harlot's Progress*	Treaty of Vienna between Austria and Britain, which recognises the Pragmatic Sanction, safeguarding Maria-Theresa's inheritance	Birth of William Cowper J.S. Bach: *Saint Mark's Passion*
1735	He inherits Thornhill's studios and sets up the Academy of St Martins in the Fields Publishes *The Rake's Progress*	Russia attacks Turkey Linnaeus starts his system of natural classification	James Thomson: *Liberty* Pope: *Moral Essays* and *Epistle To Dr Arbuthnot*

retrospect), these Whig grandees, who lived like princes, were anathema. Accordingly, they attacked the government of the day and its supporters in brilliant satires. The world of Hogarth's satirical engravings was also the world of Pope's devastating satires such as *The Dunciad,* a quotation from which appears in Hogarth's picture *The Distressed Poet* (page 10).

Hogarth, who had grown up in the narrow streets and near-slums of London, was a more typical Englishman than either Swift (born in Dublin) or Pope, who was a Catholic and therefore an outsider in a Protestant country. Equally, Hogarth did not move in court circles until late in his life, reinforcing his sense of being - and representing - an ordinary beef-eating, independent sort of Englishman, who rejects foreign fashions. Significantly, his first successful oil painting was *The Beggar's Opera* (page 4), depicting John Gay's burlesque of the Italian operas produced by Handel, that cosmopolitan composer so popular at court - but not with the country.

Such moralisingly English attitudes made Hogarth a natural friend and ally of writers not linked with the Whig aristocracy, such as Henry Fielding or Samuel Richardson. Not necessarily Tories, they still rejected the new, unabashed commercialism of the age, which reached its extreme in 1720 in the South Sea Bubble - a speculative boom in the South Sea Trading Company, which drove its shares up to an insanely inflated level before they crashed to almost nothing. This early example of stock market fever benefited a

1736	Becomes a governor of St Bartholomew's (the Foundling Hospital) where he paints frescoes for the great staircase	Christian missionaries banned from China, which closes itself off against the world	Dr Johnson: *Voyage To Abyssinia* Henry Fielding: *The Historical Register* William Kent building Holkham Hall Voltaire: *The Prodigy*
1740	Attacks the idea of a French-style Royal Academy Paints many portraits, including *Captain Coram*	Start of the War of the Austrian Succession; Frederick II, the new king of Prussia, seizes Silesia from Maria-Theresa of Austria Britain allies with Austria against France and Prussia	Samuel Richardson: *Pamela* Thomson: *Rule Britannia* James Gibbs builds the Fellows' Building at King's College, Cambridge
1744	Paints *Marriage A La Mode*	Prussia, which had earlier made peace, re-enters war against Austria	Death of Alexander Pope Dr Johnson: *Life Of Richard Savage*
1748	Second trip to France. Arrested at Calais for spying; paints *Calais Gate or The Roast Beef Of Old England*	Peace of Aix-la-Chapelle ends War of Austrian Succession. Prussia keeps Silesia, otherwise status quo restored	Thomas Gainsborough: *Mr And Mrs Andrews* Gibbs builds the Radcliffe Library, Oxford
1753	Publishes *The Analysis Of Beauty*, where he expounds his aesthetic based on serpentine lines	Influence of Madame Pompadour at its height in France British Museum started by government purchase of Sloane Collection	Joshua Reynolds: *Commodore Keppel* Dr Johnson working on his Dictionary Appearance of the third volume of the *Encyclopédie,* edited by Diderot
1757	Becomes Serjeant Painter to the King	William Pitt becomes Prime Minister Admiral Byng executed for losing Minorca Clive wins Battle of Plassey and conquers Bengal	David Hume: *Natural History Of Religion* Birth of William Blake Handel: *The Triumph Of Truth*
1762	Publishes *The Times* series, attacking John Wilkes and other former radical allies	Catherine II (the Great) becomes Empress of Russia	J-J Rousseau: *The Social Contract* Oliver Goldsmith: *The Citizen Of The World* Tiepolo works at the Royal Palace, Madrid
1764	Dies in London 25 October	France hands over Canada, Louisiana and the Antilles to Britain according to the terms of the Peace of Paris Wilkes expelled from House of Commons	Goldsmith: *The Traveller* Voltaire: *Philosophical Dictionary* Horace Walpole: *The Castle Of Otranto*

very few at the expense of the great many, some of whom lost all their savings.

This boom and bust was possible because England had developed the first truly modern banking system and stock exchange at the end of the 17th century. The Bank of England was incomparably superior to its rivals abroad. Such institutions helped propel Britain to supremacy in trade and commerce around the world, but at home they accentuated the contrast between rich and poor, especially in London, already the greatest city in Europe and growing explosively. It was the people of this booming, uncertain city, whom Hogarth depicted.

A REPORTER'S EYE

Hogarth's most famous and probably his most successful works are the satirical series *The Harlot's Progress, The Rake's Progress* (pages 6-8) *Marriage A La Mode* (pages 18-22) and *Beer Street, Gin Lane*. In all of them he is telling a story with a wealth of vividly observed detail of the London he saw around him, swarming with every specimen of humanity. He drew London's coffee-houses and taverns, its elegance and its squalor, its gaiety and its violence, but his vision would be unbearably drab if he had not crammed his pictures with comic incidents, revelling in his attacks with a schoolboyish glee.

For example, in *The Marriage Contract* (page 18), the portrait of the Earl on the left is an absurd parody of Louis XIV on the battlefield, the mirror has a gorgon's head (which traditionally turned the viewer to stone) in its centre while, visible through the window, a vast new mansion (in the Palladian style, of course) reveals exactly why the Earl is marrying off his son to the merchant's daughter - money. All is depicted with a bubbling elegant zest that is more typical of the Rococo age than the

xenophobic Hogarth would probably have cared to acknowledge. This zest is equally apparent in early works such as *Masquerades And Operas* (page 4) or late works like *The Bench* (page 3) of 34 years later, where the judges slumber heavily in the sleep of justice. (Hogarth would have known Pope's famous lines "And wretches hang that jurymen may dine"). These two engravings at the beginning and near the end of his career reveal Hogarth's satirical eye - just as sharp in the later satire as the first, despite his appointment as Serjeant painter the year before, which might have been expected to moderate his satires; but his technique has advanced dramatically. These corpulent magistrates are more fully drawn than the vivid but slight figures in the early engraving. This advance is even more apparent in his oil paintings.

Hogarth's early portraits such as *The Strode Family* (page 12) are competent but essentially unadventurous works, painted for the normal financial reasons. With his portrait of Captain Coram, however (page 14) he attempted something far grander. The painting is as much French as it is English in overall tone and spirit; the almost regal grandeur of the setting, with a great column soaring above Coram, and his chair placed like a throne looking out to sea, recall one of the portraits of the French court at Versailles - Hyacinthe Rigaud's grandiose portrait of Samuel Bernard but Hogarth humanised the chilly French portrait.

The same humanity is evident in his paintings of children such as *The Graham Children*, although Hogarth seldom managed to avoid a certain awkwardness when potraying children. To an artist of the Age of Reason, childish irrationality was not easily caught. His portraits of Garrick continue this development - with suitable melodrama; Garrick was a Shakespearean actor (page 24-25). His own self-portrait (page 1)

emphasised his Englishness (with a bulldog on the right and the works of Shakespeare in the centre) but was in fact influenced by Rembrandt's self-portraits.

His mature style reached its peak in the undramatic portraits of his servants (page 28), where he depicted their essential humanity in a way no earlier English painter had attempted; it recalls too in its total lack of pretension Rembrandt's wonderful later portraits.

A PAINTER WITHOUT HEIRS?

A genuinely English school of painting did emerge by the mid-18th century, but it did not reject traditional academic French or Italian art in favour of an art based on observation of street life, as Hogarth had hoped. Its leading painters, Thomas Gainsborough and Joshua Reynolds, followed Hogarth chronologically, but not in any way stylistically. Both looked to Italian models (although Gainsborough never left England), both pampered the nobility by making them look even more elegant than they were. Neither was English and urban in Hogarth's sense; Reynolds was consciously academic and classical, Gainsborough lyrically pastoral.

Richard Wilson, another great landscape painter of the mid-18th century, was even more indebted to his Italian experiences than Reynolds; in his canvases, the spirit of the Roman *campagna* (countryside) almost overwhelms the English landscape. Later painters were either essentially rural, like Constable, or incorporated the classical tradition before transcending it, like Turner.

Hogarth therefore has only one obvious group of successors in later Georgian England - Gilray and Cruickshank, the great cartoonists of the early 19th century. But Hogarth was more than just a satirist and therefore stands alone - the first truly great and thoroughly English painter.